Shaping Hearts and Minds

Why It Matters Where Your Child Goes to School

**MONICA WHATLEY WITH
DR. SHAWN WHATLEY**

D1409207

Published in 2016 by
Eagle and Child Books
Toronto
www.eagleandchildbooks.com

ISBN 978-0-9947376-0-1 (paperback)

Cataloguing-in-Publication Data available from Library and Archives Canada.

Cover Photograph: Hilary McLaughlin
Cover & Book Design: Dave Jumaquio

TABLE OF CONTENTS

Preface

Many Christian parents worry about their children's education, especially in North America.

We want schools that will give our kids a solid base and, ideally, an edge. We need our children to be able to think critically and to skillfully navigate twenty-first century waters as technology develops and society changes. We hope to find a school that provides a positive, moral, and preferably Christian environment.

Education shapes the future of our whole society—our children's future. School matters: we are right to worry about educational choices. As followers of Christ, education's impact is extensive and potentially eternal.

Shaping Hearts and Minds offers the essentials of classical Christian education—the education that is making a resurgence across North America.

This book offers a glimpse at what your children are being taught in today's public schools, why it's not ideal, and how their education can be better.

As you learn about classical Christian education, you may experience some of the same emotions we first had: a mixture of confusion and frustration, followed by a growing enthusiasm and passion.

This book will likely make you wish you had known about classical Christian education long ago.

CHAPTER ONE

A Snapshot

Sweet-churned butter melts into warmed tea biscuits. The sounds of clinking silverware tinkle through the air as children enjoy roast beef in makeshift period costumes.

Hieroglyphic names etched in mud pies comprise a collection from the yard. Markings, like those of early Egyptians, line tea-stained journals.

A model Milky Way hangs from the ceiling while Earth rests barely visible, prompting one to ask, "Who am *I*?"

Clerks attract buyers to their tables on Market Day, eager to make a return on their investments and still purchase others' goods.

Excitement rises over whether Plato or Aristotle takes the debate. Both make excellent cases.

This all happens at school.

Each of these lessons inspires learning. Similar scenarios weave in the Socratic method and logic, stories of ancient Greek and Roman civilizations, and an introduction to great literature, culture, and exceptional people, like Homer, Galileo, Gutenberg, and da Vinci.

More importantly, these lessons help children reflect on the past, present, and future. Such lessons confront them with the limits of their own minds.

They learn **to gain perspective**: a philosophy, a worldview, a way to see the world.

Classical education seeks to teach expansive knowledge and crucial skills through an integrated approach so these knowledge and skills become meaningful and useful.

Did we lose you at the word classical? No one wants to be *classical* in today's society.

Modern is better, right?

But what does "modern education" really look like? We will say more about this later on.

Classical does not mean antiquated, rustic, or obscurantist. In fact, classical knowledge is not limited to the last decade or century of modern perspective but seeks to understand what has been revealed to man throughout history.

Furthermore, *classical* does not ignore the aid of modern technology but actively uses technology as a tool, which helps to communicate and practice, or leverage, knowledge. Technology supports students as they begin to understand centuries of knowledge. Modern technology's uses become purposeful, as students are able to synthesize information quickly and effectively.

Classically trained students take in much more information than their non-classically trained peers. Primary-aged students eagerly point out the countries of the world, chant math facts, recite spelling and grammar rules, and encounter great works of literature. They "meet" Alexander the Great, Achilles, Julius Caesar, and Constantine and can talk about the Greeks, Romans, and early Jews with confidence.

These primary students can have a better understanding of the foundation of Western culture than most high school students today.

Many parents welcome the opportunity to have really "smart" kids. Imagine the dinner party where your child quotes Aristotle or Augustine or can speak on the Peloponnesian War, the early Mayans, or Mark Antony with ease.

But that is not what classical education is all about. Although "really smart kids" is a benefit of classical education, it is not the end goal.

When classical education is uniquely Christian, as it has been for hundreds of years, it weaves together subjects based on truth as revealed in God's Word, thus changing the student's perspective forever.

The purpose of a classical Christian education is not just to shape minds. More importantly, it shapes the heart.

It fosters a desire for Jesus Christ first so that children become more like Him, learning to love what He *loves*. Practice turns to habit, and love for the good and the true *grows*. Hearts change as these children become authentic followers of Jesus.

Out of all of this flows a different behaviour than what is found in the usual classroom setting. Students who follow Christ are led by His example.

Classical Christian education also teaches children how to think.

It builds a lens through which children see the world. Students do not merely absorb anything they are taught. They learn to see through the lens and to appreciate knowledge in light of a larger understanding. They learn *how* to think first by realizing the limits of their own understandings and gain perspective in the process.

Students learn chunks of Scripture by heart and experience it in context. Faith and learning are intertwined, not separate.

Ultimately, classically trained students learn to critically analyze arguments and eloquently defend their faith. They gain a clear purpose for their lives: to serve God with all their hearts and minds.

True classical Christian education engages.

It inspires.

It shapes what students love.

It equips and challenges students *how* to think.

Classical education cultivates lifetime learners. These students grow to love scholarship and continue to develop their own learning far beyond formal schooling years.

Classical education is likely very different from how you were educated. And after seeing it up close, you will want it for your own kids.

You might even wish you could go back to school.

CHAPTER TWO

The Heart: Why Knowledge and Worldview Don't Cut It

We can send our kids to top-rated schools. They might outperform their peers on standardized tests and become walking encyclopaedias.

They have access to virtually everything man knows today. With more knowledge at their fingertips than ever before, are our kids prepared for the future?

> Above all else, guard your heart, for everything you do flows from it.
>
> (PROVERBS 4:23)

Classical Christian education goes beyond telling students all there is to know. It reaches past the production of students who know how to think. It even supersedes teaching students character or virtue.

The ultimate core of classical Christian education is to form the students first, shaping who they are and what they love, because:

> The entire object of true education is to make people not merely to do the right things, but to enjoy them; not merely industrious, but to love industry; not merely just, but to hunger and thirst after justice.
>
> (JOHN RUSKIN)[1]

James K. A. Smith, in *Desiring the Kingdom*, writes that what "defines us is what we *love*."[2]

What do you love?

If "our ultimate love/desire is shaped by practices, not ideas that are merely communicated to us," then we as parents have an incredible responsibility.[3]

What are we communicating to our kids?

Are we telling them that hockey, or basketball, or soccer trumps church? Are we showing them that money should just be spent on ourselves? What do we tell them through what we practice?

Social media. The mall. Sports. Entertainment. Smith says these are "practices" or forms of "worship" that shape the way we think and act today. Subconscious messages stream in at breakneck speed. Our worldview forms as we practice these habits because our "orientation to the world is shaped from the body up more than from the head down. Liturgies aim our love to different ends precisely by training our hearts through our bodies."[4]

Will we be surprised, then, if our kids choose sports over church during university? Or choose Sunday as a day of errands?

Practices shape what we love and ultimately define us.

"Our hearts," as Augustine said, "are restless till they find rest in [God]."[5] We are created to long for the kingdom. James K. A. Smith says that we take far more in by feeling than thinking. Our "worldview is more a matter of the imagination than the intellect," so building a Christian worldview based on intellect is not enough.[6] We can learn all the right answers through the right lens and still be a lover of the world.

In reality, it's not what we know, but what we practice. It's our Christian worship, and it comes before worldview.

We love it before we understand or know it.

> Discipleship and formation are . . . a matter of developing a Christian know-how that intuitively 'understands' the world in the light of the fullness of the gospel. And insofar as an understanding is implicit in practice, the practices of Christian worship are crucial—the sine qua non—for developing a distinctly Christian understanding of the world.[7]

A classical Christian school trains the heart through practice. Practices form habits, habits shape our character, and character forms our future.

Classical Christian education fosters a desire for the kingdom in these frail, earthly bodies. Students grow in their desire for the kingdom as they follow Christ, first with their hearts, and then "everything [they] do flows from it" (Proverbs 4:23).

Knowledge is put into focus.

CHAPTER 3

What Is Classical Christian Education, Anyway?

Now that you have a taste of the true purpose of classical Christian education, it will help to understand **what** it is.

Language arts, social studies, science, math, and physical education pack modern, mainstream school schedules. Teachers transfer information in separate packages, stacking one on top of another like Lego blocks.

> Although we often succeed in teaching our pupils "subjects," we fail lamentably on the whole in teaching them how to think: they learn everything, except the art of learning.[8]

Again, classical education seeks to train the heart and teach students *how* to think while renewing the art of learning.

It is different from other methods, techniques, or philosophies found in most schools today.

Christopher Perrin provides a summary:

> **Classical (and Christian) education** is a traditional approach to education that blends Christian theology with the historic curriculum and pedagogy of the seven liberal arts in order to produce societal leaders characterized by wisdom, virtue and eloquence.[9]

Classical education labours to truly understand the ideas of Western civilization found in the Great Books written throughout history. The seven liberal arts—grammar, logic, rhetoric, arithmetic, geometry, astronomy, and music—are taught traditionally. Classical Christian education aims to cultivate wisdom, virtue, and the search for truth in a reflective, Christ-centered environment.

Perrin also adds that classical education:

- Trains one's desires and understanding
- Values discussion and contemplation
- Encourages an understanding of the past
- Adapts to discoveries and new information

- Builds a foundation that supports any profession
- Trains leaders
- Partners with the church[10]

You won't be surprised to hear that history plays a large role in classical education.

We know about history through the writings of the people who went before us. Plato, Homer, and Virgil enlighten us on Greek and Roman experiences and thought. We read about our roots of freedom, justice, faith, beauty, and civil rights among the Great Books.

Why? Because classicists believe that only in building upon the past can we prepare for the future.

Like Christian thinkers before us, we can take the richness of the past and learn from it.

Western civilization, or the embodiment of Western culture's social behaviour, values, and ideas, gave us most of the science, literature, art, democracy, and commerce that we depend on each day. Western civilization came out of a Judeo-Christian understanding of the world.[11]

Since the time of Plato, Western civilization declared the **reality** of truth, beauty, and goodness.

The Christian understanding that God himself **is that reality**, and is therefore the essence of truth, beauty, and goodness, is what led to the rise of the university in medieval Europe. It was called a university because of the debate that arose over whether we could actually know these universals or whether they were simply nominal.[12]

This declaration stands in stark contrast to modern expressions of skepticism about the reality of truth, beauty, and goodness, as we note in the philosophies of **relativism** (knowledge, truth, and morality are not absolutes), **pragmatism** (knowledge, truth, and morality are only useful, not real, and can therefore be ignored if required) and **solipsism** (self is all that is known to exist).

Classicists believe that a recovery of the tradition of wisdom and delight in the good, the true, and the beautiful found in God can help to reverse the move of Western civilization away from its roots in Western culture. Past civilizations, and especially Christian values, helped build Western culture.

Progressives, by definition, seek to change society and build new social structures. They minimize historical influences as they work to restructure culture.

We need to agree on the true, the good, and the beautiful or we put the pillars of our culture at great risk.

Classicists depend on the Christian Scriptures. They contain some of the earliest writings on major themes that flow through human history.

The Bible addresses sibling rivalry, infidelity, slavery, genocide, murder, and greed. It offers some of the earliest explanations for geopolitical corruption and national suffering. It uncovers the motivations behind war and oppression and offers political solutions that lead to peace and prosperity.

Relationships, a core feature of human society, are displayed in mature detail in the Bible. Readers learn about interactions between siblings, parents, lovers, tribes, and nations.

The Bible addresses money, trade, commerce, and investment. It defines work and rest, industry and leisure.

Surely, no educated person can assume himself to be so without thorough exposure to the Scriptures.

The Bible is our "map."

The Scriptures provide a detailed map for our journey with certain routes clearly blocked and others unnecessarily difficult. We have an idea of which paths get to our destination without repeating others' mistakes.

We can also learn from others who have worked to understand the past and God's truth as revealed throughout time. In a classical school, one reads Homer, Aristotle, Virgil, Augustine, Bunyan, and C. S. Lewis. By the Holy Spirit, through God's Word, we use these texts to recognize the preservation of our culture in its greatest form. Truth is understood in Augustine, and morality is reflected in Aristotle. These and other authors wrote books that grapple with foundational values and ideas.

We believe the Bible is the greatest of all books.

A list of Great Books (expanded on in *The Well-Trained Mind*) might include but is not limited to:

Epic of Gilgamesh (circa 2500 BC)
The Iliad and *The Odyssey*, by Homer (circa 850 BC)
Medea, by Euripides (circa 431 BC)
Republic - Symposium, by Plato (circa 387 BC)

On Poetics, Ethics, by Aristotle (384-322 BC)

De republic, by Cicero (54 BC)

The Aeneid, by Virgil (circa AD 30)

The Wars of the Jews, by Josephus (circa 68)

Confessions and City of God, by Augustine (circa 400)

Beowulf (circa 1000)

Aquinas: Selected Writings, (circa 1273)

The Inferno, by Dante (1320)

The Canterbury Tales, by Chaucer (circa 1400)

The Prince, by Machiavelli (1513)

Utopia, by More (1516)

Divine Meditations, by Donne (circa 1635)

Principles of Philosophy, by Descartes (1644)

Paradise Lost, by Milton (1664)

Pensees, by Pascal (1670)

Pilgrim's Progress, by Bunyan (1678)

"An Essay Concerning Human Understanding," by Locke (1690)

"The Social Contract," by Rousseau (1762)

"Critique of Pure Reason," by Kant (1781)

"The Rights of Man," by Paine (1792)

Frankenstein, by Shelley (1818)

"Self-Reliance," by Emerson (1844)

Communist Manifesto, by Marx and Engels (1848)

Walden, by Thoreau (1854)

Crime and Punishment, by Dostoyevsky (1856)

On the Origin of Species, by Darwin (1859)

Great Expectations, by Dickens (1861)

Thus Spoke Zarathustra, by Nietzsche (1883)

The Interpretation of Dreams, by Freud (1900)

"The Innocence of Father Brown," by Chesterton (1911)

"A Poem with Notes and Grace Notes," by Frost (1924)

Mein Kampf, by Hitler (1939)

Animal Farm, by Orwell (1945)

The Diary of Anne Frank, by Frank (1947)

Invisible Man, by Ellison (1952)

Mere Christianity, by Lewis (1952)

"Why We Can't Wait," by King Jr. (1964)[13]

Some might feel overwhelmed by this abridged list.

Or perhaps uncomfortable.

This is expected, but there is an important purpose to this exposure . . .

CHAPTER 4

Insulate, Immerse, or Inoculate?

Hitler? Nietzsche? Machiavelli? Freud? Why would we want our children spending any time on some of these writers from the list of "greats" in the last chapter?

Rather than providing a protective bubble from this information and **insulating** students from these ideas, or **immersing** them before they are ready, the classical Christian school chooses to **inoculate** them. Classical Christian education intentionally exposes students and gives them the tools to navigate through the difficult issues they will eventually encounter.[14]

Think of it this way:

If you are going to visit another country, you might prepare your children by ensuring they have the appropriate vaccines before you leave.

Alternatively, you might not go in the first place. You might shelter your children, keeping them home with the idea that they never need to be exposed.

Or you can send them without vaccines and immerse them in the country right from the start.

Another way to think of it is by considering the danger of water, with drowning as the second leading cause of death, behind birth defects, among one to four-year-olds.[15] Knowing your kids could drown, you could isolate them from water—not expose or tell them about it, live far away from any source, and hope and pray they never have access.

Wanting a better program for my kids, I* attempted to do this with our children at first. I homeschooled them; I didn't want them exposed too early. I planned to expose them myself, but they never seemed quite "ready" . . . until their friends took the lead.

---

*"Me" or "I" throughout the book refers to Monica as the primary author.

Or, because water is dangerous, you could immerse them right away. Since they need to know how to swim, you can throw • them in the deep end as a toddler, unsupervised, so they can learn how to deal with the danger.

Many of my friends believe this is the best way. If they need to survive in the world, they need to start practicing from Day One.

Lastly, since water is dangerous, you could inoculate or enroll them in swimming lessons. Under the watchful eye of a qualified instructor, they can progress from beginner to expert. They will learn how to navigate deep water well and to avoid possible danger: diving in uninspected areas, swimming alone, becoming vulnerable to undertows, etc.

Instead of insulating children in order to shelter them or immersing them before they are ready, classical Christian schools inoculate students by intentionally introducing them to ideas and information with guidance from a knowledgeable instructor so that they are better prepared for what they will face.

The classical approach to education works to help students comprehend the writing of the people who influenced human thinking throughout time.

Understanding Hitler's philosophy helps us see how his ideas became choices—choices that led to some of the worst atrocities in modern history. We learn so that we do not make the same decisions ourselves. As Edmund Burke memorably said,

> Those who don't know history are destined to repeat it.

When we are completely ignorant of the past, we make the same mistakes as those before us.

Classical education labours to equip students with extensive knowledge, but knowledge is not a goal in itself. Many systems pass down information and teach children what to think.

Again, with the primary focus on training the heart first, classically educated students are taught *how* to think—how to synthesize an entire history of learning. This is done where thoughts and knowledge are understood through a lens of Christ's work on earth, His work to renew all of creation.

Students consider *why* and *how* events took place, theories are discussed, and ideas are passed on by reading these great works.

Through this, they gain clear perspective.

CHAPTER 5

The Process

Now that you know more of what classical Christian education is, let's look at **how** it works.

Learning to think through and synthesize an entire history of learning may sound overwhelming, but the process is quite simple.

Classical education aligns with students' natural intellectual development. It is often divided into different stages, called the *Trivium*, or three paths, based on the first three liberal arts: grammar, logic, and rhetoric.[16]

The first stage, the **Grammar Stage**, usually consists of grades K through 5 or 6 and lays foundational groundwork. Young kids have brains like sponges. They can fill their minds with an incredible amount of content, and songs, chants, and rhymes help children commit these facts to memory. Information, whether it is the math facts, countries of the world, or spelling rules, will stay with them for the rest of their lives, so this is the period of building knowledge.

Stage two, the **Logic Stage**, typically starts in Grade 6 or 7. Students start to think independently and want to understand, not just take in, information. With a strong base of knowledge from the Grammar Stage, they begin to think more abstractly and ask *why* and *how*. Their perspectives widen and they start to recognize connections throughout the content, understanding why important events in history took place. Students become ready for the application of formal logic and learn how to support an idea and critically analyze literature, as their grasp of the art of argumentation develops.

The third stage of the Trivium is the **Rhetoric Stage**, which generally occurs in the high school grades. Using their strong foundations of knowledge and skills in logic from earlier grades, students in the Rhetoric Stage learn to express ideas clearly and effectively to others. They gain confidence to think for themselves and are able to share their worldviews eloquently through their speech and writing.

Although each stage has a specific focus, knowledge and skills are not confined to a particular level. Third grade students will study the logic of a theory in science, while high school students will focus on memorizing facts pivotal to a concept.

However, the classical Christian focus is not limited to the three paths of liberal arts: grammar, logic, and rhetoric. Cultivation of moral virtue and the mathematical arts of arithmetic, geometry, astronomy, and music, or the *Quadrivium* ("four paths"), are also traditionally part of the classical school because "the ancients believed [all] seven 'arts' were not merely subjects to be mastered, but sure and certain ways of forming in the soul the intellectual virtue necessary for acquiring true wisdom."[17]

The Trivium acts as a framework for integrated knowledge. Subjects are not separate from each other; science thrives throughout history and language while art is reflected in geography and math. Understanding information in its greater context makes it more meaningful and useful.[18]

The Christian faith is a unique, historic faith. God not only created space and time, but can be seen "in the things that have been made" (Romans 1:20). He also entered human history as a man and has continued to act in history. This is clearly evident as He has worked through the Holy Spirit in His people for millennia. History is the theatre of God's providence, and a careful study demonstrates the effect of His kingdom reign on mankind: "In Him, all things hold together" (Colossians 1:17).[19]

The classical approach uses history as its core, organizing literature, language, geography, science, art, music, and math around it. History is often broken down into periods: Ancients, Middle Ages, Renaissance and Reformation, and Modern Times. Ancient times are explored in Grade 1 or 2, and students move through the historical cycle chronologically, not in fragmented leaps like other curricula.

Latin is also usually part of the classical school's content. It is considered foundational for English; a large portion of English words come from Latin roots.[20] Learning Latin helps classical students grasp English language structure and aids in the learning of Latin-based Romance languages. Students studying Latin for a minimum of two years score significantly higher on the SAT.[21] Latin also helps students understand great historical works.

Classical educators masterfully interweave this rich content through their own thorough grasp of it. In a classical school, one will often find **not only** the basic provincial or state teacher qualifications, but masters or doctorate levels of scholarship as classical teachers exemplify the lifelong learner.

From the content-rich early grades, through the period of questioning and greater understanding in the middle grades, to the confidence and competence required to share and support one's ideas in high school, a classical Christian education helps the student take from the past to build the future using the lens of a Christian worldview.

As children learn how to think, they can enter into the "Great Conversation," Robert Hutchins' summary of the dialogue between the world's greatest thinkers throughout time:

> The tradition of the West is embodied in the Great Conversation that began in the dawn of history and that continues to the present day.[22]

These thinkers referred to their predecessors' work, carrying on the conversation throughout history.

A classical approach to education is aimed to prepare the child's heart and mind to join the Great Conversation one step at a time.

CHAPTER 6

Lost Treasure

Socrates. Plato. Augustine. Aquinas. Pascal. Hildegard. Galileo. Archimedes. Einstein. Joan of Arc. Copernicus. Columbus. Shakespeare. Darwin. Elizabeth I. Luther. Newton.

Likely, you have heard these names. Perhaps you even understand their significance.

These people influenced society in a timeless way. These are among the classically educated, and this list goes on.

Fathers of Canadian and American confederation, John A. Macdonald, George Etienne Cartier, and Thomas Jefferson, also had a similarly strong foundation. The schools in early North America were typically classical Christian schools.

[They] studied the Bible in its original Hebrew and Greek, and they read Homer's Iliad in Greek, Tacitus' histories in Latin, as well as studying John Calvin's Institutes of the Christian Religion.[23]

Most of the greatest influential thinkers, scientists, politicians, mathematicians, and Christian leaders throughout time were classically educated.

They depended on those before them to help them find their way. Galilei quoted Plato. Newton referred to Gassendi. Discovery built on understanding passed throughout time.[24]

Even pagan philosophers reflected on truth, beauty, and goodness in their writing because they recognized their value to society. Great thinkers throughout time influenced thought because they understood where man had been and was going.

Most of these great people rested on the same foundational core of a successful society that was passed down from generation to generation. Their classical education enabled them to dramatically change the society of their time, which ultimately shaped our own society.

They weren't just great thinkers; they became great influencers of change.

Students have the potential to gain perspective through the study of these influential people including:

- The "Father of History," Herodotus.
- The "Father of Western Medicine" and creator of the Hippocratic Oath, Hippocrates of Kos.
- The Greek philosopher who shaped thinking on ethics, logic, and philosophy, Aristotle.
- The military leader who grew one of the largest empires in ancient times in his short lifetime, Alexander the Great.
- The talented Greek inventor and mathematician, Archimedes.
- The ruler who changed the form of government and built a foundation for Western civilization, Julius Caesar.
- The leader who was not afraid to ensure Christianity flourished in the expansive Roman Empire, Constantine the Great.
- The "Renaissance Man" who showed genius across the curriculum in art, music, math, science, and engineering, Leonardo da Vinci.

- The "Father of Modern Science," or the man who was willing to challenge the belief of where Earth fit in the universe, Galileo Galilei.
- The brilliant scientist who made discoveries throughout the Scientific Revolution, Isaac Newton.
- The philosopher who influenced thought on freedom and liberty, John Stuart Mill.
- The president who abolished slavery and led his country through civil war, Abraham Lincoln.

We owe our grasp of science, our philosophy and ethics, our understanding of language and history, and our laws and freedom today to people like these who built our foundation.

This does not mean that everything they said was true or good. We need to sift through what they said, guided by the light of revelation.

But we cannot do this if we are not exposed to it.

These and other influential people spent a great deal of time thinking, writing and learning, and building upon past theories and ideas—many grappling with issues we struggle with today, such as justice, faith, truth, civil rights, and freedom.

This was done through the filter of two thousand years of learning in Western civilization and in the conversation that has taken place throughout the centuries.

The conversation is being cut off in modern education, without us even realizing it.

CHAPTER 7

A Good Enough Education

Forget about Peter, Plato, and Persia for a minute. Perhaps you think your child doesn't need a better education. Perhaps you think you received a "good enough" education and your child is getting an even better one.

Consider this:

Test scores are out. Your child earns a Level 3, the local average. You sigh in relief.

At least she's not behind.

Better yet, she lands a 4, and you hold your head a little higher.

My child is pretty smart, you think. *She's doing better than the majority of other students her age in this country.*

But what does this score really tell you?

How *is* the average student in the country doing? What skills has he or she really mastered? What does the average student know?

Does your child know more or less than you did at her age? How would she measure up to your parents at the same stage? Your grandparents?

Perhaps you conclude that your child must be quite advanced:

Schooling is progressive. Education is getting better and better, as we perfect the art of learning. Besides, the people before us knew so much less than we do today.

Right?

In 1984, Gary Ingersoll and Carl Smith surveyed over four thousand 6–14 year olds and noted that this age group's active written vocabulary was reduced by more than half, from 25,000 to 10,000 words within a forty-year period. The study reiterated "the understanding of [a] sentence is enhanced by the knowledge of component words," affecting students' reading ability.[25]

The Organisation for Economic Cooperation and Development surveyed a minimum of five thousand people in thirty-three countries worldwide, assessing basic literacy, numeracy, and problem-solving in 2013. Among 16–24 year olds, the United States scored second to last in literacy. In numeracy and problem-solving, the United States came in last. Canada's scores for this age group were also below the average. And this only compares our educated to other countries today—not to those educated throughout history.[26]

In 2013, a University of Amsterdam study revealed that western nations have lost an average of fourteen IQ points since the Victorian age.[27]

What does this suggest to us?

The tragedy today is that we don't even know what we don't know.

We are ignorant of our ignorance.

We think that we have received a solid foundation ourselves. Perhaps we have done a little better than members of our social group. Maybe we are in a higher tier of the educated. A dentist? A Master's of Business Administration? A lawyer? We may be *experts* in our fields.

For most of the twentieth century, education has been designed to create *experts* in a single field. Modern jobs require content expertise.

But as experts, how good is our overall knowledge base? Is there truth to Will Rogers' statement?

> [There is] nothing as stupid as an educated man if you get him off the thing he was educated in.[28]

If we consider the change in education over the last fifty or hundred years, we find a notable trend. The Industrial Revolution created a need to educate workers, not thinkers.[29] Job opportunities multiplied, and workers needed skills to use and develop technology.

Education shifted its focus from teaching students how to think to teaching them how to get along in industry.

For centuries, classical education had produced some of the greatest thinkers of all time. But in order to keep up with the demands of industrialization, skills needed to be learned quickly. Workers had to get along. Order and productivity became paramount.

The easiest way to do this was to trim off some "unnecessary" content from the curricula, such as the liberal arts: history, music, art, etc.

Why consider ideas when it distracts from the task at hand?

Why think of beauty when you can focus on skill?

Over the last hundred years, the curricula began to emphasize math, science, and social studies until very little else remained. Math and science, treated as objective and irrefutable, removed one's need to synthesize information.

Students were not required to *think* because they were trained to *do*.

The liberal arts became "fat" meant for trimming, leaving education focused on science, math, and social studies.

A trimmed-down curricula made room for **scientism**, the belief that science is the best or only source of true knowledge. Students embraced scientism without knowing anything different.

Science must start with thought, reflection, and ultimately *guessing* before it can produce the concrete, technological wonders we enjoy. Science starts in something outside science: in imagination, thought, and reflection.

Students graduate able to perform tasks but are less capable of thinking for themselves.

This shift in focus dramatically affected modern education—our own education.

Are we better for it?

Read on and decide for yourself.

CHAPTER 8

How Much Do You Know?

Perhaps you have a college diploma or a university degree. You may have even earned a masters or Ph.D. Maybe, you are one of the experts mentioned in the last chapter.

What you are about to do should not be difficult then.

How many of these questions can you answer completely and correctly? (Put away your smartphone!)

GRAMMAR

1. Give nine rules for the use of Capital Letters.

2. What are the Principal Parts of a verb? Give Principal Parts of do, lie, lay and run.

MATH

1. District No. 33 has a valuation of $35,000. What is the necessary levy to carry on a school seven months at $50 per month, and have $104 for incidentals?

2. Find the interest of $512.60 for 8 months and 18 days at 7 per cent.

ORTHOGRAPHY

1. Define the following prefixes and use in connection with a word: Bi, dis, mis, pre, semi, post, non, inter, mono, super.

2. Use the following correctly in sentences: Cite, site, sight, fane, fain, feign, vane, vain, vein, raze, raise, rays.

GEOGRAPHY

1. Name all the republics of Europe and give capital of each.

2. Why is the Atlantic Coast colder than the Pacific in the same latitude?

BIOLOGY

1. Where are the saliva, gastric juice, and bile secreted? What is the use of each in digestion?

2. How does nutrition reach the circulation?

Can you answer all of these questions correctly with confidence?

This is only a tiny portion of an eighth-grade exam from 1895. You can find the original document in the collection of the Smoky Valley Genealogy Society.[30]

Perhaps you know all the answers to one of the areas' questions. Maybe you are a health professional and biology is your bailiwick. Or maybe you are an *expert* in math or geography.

The reality is, few adults today would be able to ace this entire eighth-grade exam.

Most of the students who took this exam in 1895 were farmers in rural Kansas. They were educated very differently than we are today.

What does this say about our education?

This exam does not even reflect the missing "fat." There are no questions about world history, philosophy, religion, languages, logic, art, or music. Students a century ago were trained in all of these.

Modern curriculum changes as the country continually brings in information about how and what students should learn. The media boldly makes its statement with headlines, such as: "Ontario's sex-ed curriculum teaches society's values, and that's good."[31]

Curriculum focuses less and less on producing independent thinkers as it works increasingly to socialize children.

Modern education assumes children depend on technology to find information.

Most everything students want to know can be found on the Internet. But the new curriculum only suggests ways to manipulate media and ignores the fact that students lack context and perspective and have not learned *how* to synthesize the information they now have access to. They also lack the tools to critique that information.

Our current society is expected to thrive when children grow up and get along with others as they work within the system. Modern education does not equip them to think for themselves or to challenge it. Central planners trim content to make more room to socialize children. This socialization trains students in values antithetical to a Christian worldview. We need to ask more about *why* and *how* and what this means for the influencers of tomorrow.

It all comes down to philosophy.

CHAPTER 9

The Culprit: Philosophy, and How It Changes Culture

Today, educators are committed to a variety of methods: inquiry-based, child-centred, play-based—all the buzzwords. They hold fast to these methods promising self-directed, independent, lifelong learners.

But, "Every pedagogy assumes and expresses an anthropology."[32]

Every approach to education presupposes an assumption about what the child is like.

Inquiry-based learning encourages students to direct their development through natural questions while the teacher acts as facilitator.

This method assumes that students have the knowledge and skills to ask key questions and then the sophistication to observe and apply new information to their understanding of the world.

Child-centred learning also moves the teacher into the facilitator role. Children choose their activities based on individual interests and "readiness." Children are able to work side-by-side independently because they determine their own program.

Child-centred learning assumes that the child is "ready" when he is interested.

> *If little Johnny doesn't want to read, he doesn't have to go to the letter table.*

In Canada, kindergarten has become more play-based as children again direct their day.[33] Letter sounds disappear as Play-Doh and blocks take centre stage in the senior kindergarten *playroom.*

Play-based learning sees education through play. It assumes that children do not need to be exposed to "direct learning" until they reach the first grade.

What are we telling these students?

That they are smart enough to figure out what and when they should be learning (and, perhaps, that they are the centre of the classroom and universe), or that they aren't smart enough to officially start learning until they reach Grade One?

Is this what we think?

Or are we keenly aware that children are human, and their natural response to these freedoms might ultimately be to do less than they are capable of? Why should they challenge themselves if no one else will?

A parent shared a story of a dinnertime conversation between little and big brothers with me. The little brother, in a classical Christian school, was talking about Bolivia. The big brother, in a public school, stated that there was no such place. The parent was surprised to hear the little brother respond, "Of course there is. Bolivia is a country in South America."

Was this something picked up through play-based, child-centred, or inquiry-based learning? No, this little brother knew the countries of South America through a classical approach and was able to point to each South American country on a map, even though he was only in junior kindergarten.

The truth is, it is remarkable how children will rise to the occasion when much is expected of them.

Recently, another fifth-grade student reflected on what he was learning in history. "Why doesn't my mom know this stuff?" he asked my fellow teacher. "How do *you* know it? It's all so interesting!"

Do we know what children are capable of? The current education system seems to think it is less and less.

Ultimately, there is a difference between the method and the philosophy of education.

Methods emphasize techniques that claim to help students excel. Philosophy describes a whole approach or perspective on how knowledge should fit together.

A philosophy of education might use many different techniques to deliver a message. These techniques may change depending on the teachers, students, or resources, but the message is constant.

What is the message of the public education system? What does it say about the child? The teacher? The parent? Or God?

Classical Christian education is centred on the philosophy that we can only know where we are going when we know where we have been.

Classically educated students have a huge knowledge base. They become socialized through exposure to classical Western content, not modern, progressive social fads.

As C. S. Lewis writes,

> Most of all, perhaps, we need an intimate knowledge of the past. Not that the past has anything magic about it, but we cannot study the future, and yet need something to set against the present, to remind us that the basic assumptions have been quite different in different periods and that much which seems certain to the uneducated is merely temporary fashion. A man who has lived in many places is not likely deceived by the local errors of his native village; the scholar has lived in many times and is therefore in some degree immune from the great cataract of nonsense that pours from the press and the microphone of his own age.[34]

By digging deeply into our past, we learn about and from the great thinkers and leaders who have gone before us. We understand the ideas and events that have shaped who we are today.

In the Scriptures, God speaks to the poor choices of man, both believer and pagan. The Bible is not afraid to talk about bad choices and sin.

Classical education is not afraid to learn from them.

Classical Christian education stands apart from other approaches today because it starts from unique assumptions that are disappearing from today's culture. Classical Christian education:

- values the foundation built by committed believers throughout the centuries.
- believes that Western culture providentially offers values and ways to implement them.
- sees a need to preserve the foundation of Western culture for our future.

What's so great about Western culture, you ask?

Plenty.

It has the best medicine, art, government, music, literature, technology, commerce, human rights, diversity, longevity, and opportunities of any civilization known to date.

Western civilization joins Greek rationality and Judeo-Christian history. To paraphrase the great English writer, G.K. Chesterton, it combines furious opposites and keeps them both furious.[35]

Modern education is based on an entirely different philosophy.

Over several hundred years, society began to throw out history and the liberal arts and came to rely on reason and science, removing God and spirituality, and ultimately man's heart and soul, from the conversation.

Throughout the seventeenth century, people tired of religious wars.[36] *God only complicated things*, so He needed to be taken out of the equation. Francis Bacon investigated nature by stripping things down to their simplest parts. The beliefs of the time essentially said,

We cannot learn about cannons and cannon balls if we get distracted with questions about why we should or should not fire cannons. Questions about right and wrong get in the way of the more important task of finding out how things work. No one can learn how to accurately fire a cannon ball by bringing religion into the armoury.

Modern education builds on the same reductionist approach. It suggests religion just distracts from the important work of fact and reason.

History just brings up historic feuds. Great literature does not add anything to the practical skills that modern students need to know, and people talk differently now.

Its solution?

Throw it all out. It's not useful anyways.

Removing Christian faith from all facets of society dramatically changes our culture and our children's environment.

So, how is this working for us?

[See Appendix A: How We Got Here in the First Place for more discussion on the history and philosophy of modern education and Appendix B: The Alternative.]

CHAPTER 10

Reaping What Was Sown

Modern education has cut off the Great Conversation through time.

Today's education believes the past is not necessary or useful because man knows more today. In fact, it believes man is progressing from the archaic beliefs of those held before us. C. S. Lewis called this *"chronological snobbery."*[37]

Modern philosophy suggests man should start his own conversation from scratch, without the outdated, constrained views of those before us.[38]

Society has redefined leadership around current icons like Bill Gates, Ellen DeGeneres, and Mark Zuckerberg. The measuring stick of what is good or right warps as our culture develops on completely different principles. These principles change as the seasons change. But they are trends that look foolish in hindsight, like bell-bottoms and mullets.

The concepts of truth, beauty, and goodness get bent to meet different ends.

Truth becomes subjective. Beauty becomes comparative. Goodness becomes relative. Pressure to promote tolerance unearths the deep roots of virtue.

The public system teaches good character and virtue by adding them as separate, isolated lessons in the academic program.[39]

Because they are not connected to a purpose, hearts are not changed, and overall student behaviour digresses. Teachers work to control classrooms of children raised on different, ever-changing principles.

Although the modern educational system sees the value of these Christian ideas, it will not recognize them as so, or assign a clear object to them. It teaches tolerance, but tolerance to what? It teaches freedom, but freedom to do what? Equality and justice for whom? Everyone? Is that possible?

It's like a child receiving an inheritance of a highly successful third-generation business. Without understanding the vision, mission, investment, sacrifice, and founding principles that made the business prosper, the child risks the whole trust.

The ignorant, arrogant child assumes he knows best. An inheritance can be squandered if it loses its foundation—its principles.

This will happen to modern society, unless the next generation learns from those before us.

Are we too busy to care?

We get swept along with modern thinking and don't even realize the unraveling of the net that holds society together. We go from activity to activity, forgetting about any time outside our own short lives. Even the most committed amongst us become self-serving.

Hezekiah, despite his father's example, was an exemplary follower of God. He knew that Judah's hardships were a result of rejecting the Lord, so "He did what was right in the eyes of the Lord" (2 Kings 18:3).

> [He] trusted in the Lord, the God of Israel, so that there was none like him among all the kings of Judah after him, nor among those who were before him. For he held fast to the Lord. He did not depart from following him, but kept the commandments that the Lord commanded Moses (2 Kings 18:5–6).

Do we hope the same will be said of us? These are high compliments.

But even after he became deathly ill and was then blessed with an additional fifteen years of renewed health, Hezekiah's pride over his military and economic strength squelched his passion for the Lord. Sadly, the words above do not describe Hezekiah at the end of his life.

In our lack of vision, just like Hezekiah, we ultimately think:

> Isn't it enough if there is peace and security as long as I live? (2 Kings 20:19).

Like modernists, we risk putting ourselves before our children's future, robbing them of their inheritance. We do not deny ourselves. Instead, we invest in the temporary, squandering the inheritance for them that was given freely to us.

Parents pour energy into their children's performances in sport or academia. This gives a false sense of security and accomplishment—a false sense of "peace and security as long as [we] live" (2 Kings 20:19). It builds a love for something other than what our hearts were designed for.

We need a radical change of direction in modern life, or we risk losing the perspective from the past forever.

The best way to influence the thinking of future generations is to restart the Great Conversation.

Classical Christian schools enable our children to ask the important questions, to learn how to process ideas, and to ultimately have something to say.

CHAPTER 11

Another Clever Devil?

*"[Evildoers] are more pained if their villa is poor than if
their life is bad, as though man's greatest good were to have
everything good except himself."*[40]

A thorough study of revelation throughout time is not enough.
A head full of knowledge and the ability to argue one's case is
extremely valuable . . . and potentially very dangerous without
virtue. According to Arthur Wellesley,

> Educate people without religion and you make them but
> clever devils.[41]

Our current culture doesn't need another clever devil. Building
one's intellect is counterproductive if one has no virtue. As
Theodore Roosevelt said,

> To educate a man in mind and not in morals is to educate a
> menace to society.[42]

Morals or "character traits" intended to shape our public-
schooled children today are not enough. Students work to
show "goodness" and "integrity" and struggle to understand
what they really mean.

Again, classical Christian education works to shape the heart.
It labours to nurture and grow the love of Christ, from whom
virtue flows.

But morals unconnected to a moral lawgiver become relative.
We look to the circumstance to decide if it is a good idea to tell
the truth. Emphasis focuses on benefits, and ethics become
situational.

Moralism insists that we can achieve righteousness with good
behaviour. Combined with modern relativism, moderns
believe that one is a better person purely because of what one
does. Improved behaviour seems to supersede the need for
sanctification.

As believers, the core to our faith—the redemptive power
of the cross of Jesus Christ—is replaced by an attempt to be

"good" people. Since "good" has become relative, it drifts and changes with time. The lines of right and wrong blur, and truth depends on the philosophy of the teacher or politician who shares it.

The core of classical Christian education is to cultivate wisdom and virtue resulting from growing in relationship with our Creator, as we understand truth as revealed throughout time.

The classically trained student's perspective is shaped as he grows in discernment, honour, eloquence, goodness, integrity, and service.

Truth, goodness, and beauty are reborn for the classical student.

The student quickly learns that the mantras of our culture, found even in Christian circles, do not fit with experience and understanding.

The student recognizes that:

He is *not* the centre of the universe.

He is *not* on the earth to serve himself.

And that it's *not* too late to live differently. God has gifted him with an incredible brain—to think, to ask questions:

How does the body reflect God's design?

How is beauty displayed in art and music?

Where do we fit in recorded and future time?

What is God's purpose for our lives?

How does God's passion for glory reflect His love for us?

The sacred and secular are not separate in the way the world wants to portray them.[43] "Bible" in a classical Christian school is not just a class taught two or three times a week to study its stories. Biblical truth is integrated throughout every area of the curricula.

The Bible is used as a window through which to see the world. Its truth gives perspective and light to understanding.

A study of virtues by those who have gone before us gives a better grasp of God's design and purpose for us.

Through their study, students see how Jesus epitomizes the virtues, and how many before us toiled to understand them: how Thomas à Kempis wrestled with goodness, how Aristotle understood wisdom and justice, how Shakespeare worked to represent love, and how Augustine studied truth.

As students engage in these works, they consider the value of these virtues and the call to see them in their own lives and share them with others.

Again, classical Christian education not only trains the child's mind, but most importantly, it trains his heart.

What can this look like?

You have already seen how the mind is changed through a program that raises the academic bar.

But what can a heart trained by years of classical Christian education look like?

Grade 12 students graduating from classical Christian schools have hearts trained by their parents, church, and school to focus on the eternal, rather than the temporary. These students serve a purpose greater than themselves. They base their decisions on a desire to bring God glory, rather than to fulfill their own passing interests or pleasures.

Students show a passion to share what they know—to go out and impact others for Christ, whether locally or abroad. They shape culture instead of letting popular culture shape them. They can articulate an attractive, thoughtful explanation of what they believe. These young men and women have a clear purpose: to serve God with all of their hearts and minds.

Is this what you want for your children?

Perhaps you have your children in public or Christian school. And you think, it can't be that bad.

My children are really doing fine, you think.

They aren't learning that 'garbage' in their school, anyway.

It's time to dispel a couple of myths.

CHAPTER 12

Myth #1: Public Education is Neutral

"To commit our children to the care of irreligious persons, is to commit lambs to the superintendency of wolves."[44]

The Mackay Committee of Ontario in 1969 stated that public teachers were required "to bring home to pupils as far as their capacity allows, the fundamental truths of Christianity and their bearing on human life and thought."[45]

Less than fifty years ago, this was public school in Ontario, Canada.

But twenty-five years ago, the Lord's Prayer was removed from Ontario schools.

After this came the progressive rejection of God and His Word.

Twenty years ago, the human rights code outlined how religious accommodation should look in Ontario schools. [46]

Five years ago, public schools struggled with what to do about Christmas.[47]

And Muslims were given class time for their prayer practice.[48]

Today's educational leaders work to promote equality and tolerance while rejecting Christianity's influence on their very foundation.

> Public schools teach religion, too—not a formal, theistic religion, but a set of values and beliefs that constitute a religion in all but name. The present arrangements abridge the religious freedom of parents who do not accept the religion taught by the public schools yet are forced to pay to have their children indoctrinated with it, and to pay still more to have their children escape indoctrination.[49]

We may not even recognize secular philosophy around and among us. We choose the public school because it gives our kids the content they need to do well in high school and university. Because the content itself seems unbiased, we expect a neutral program. We teach our children about faith from home and trust that they do not receive any spiritual training in a public school.

But removing God from the program is far from neutral.

This "neutral" education promotes another worldview: one that says God is irrelevant, morals are relative, and truth is subjective.

> The school system that ignores God teaches its pupils to ignore God; and this is not neutrality. It is the worst form of antagonism, for it judges God to be unimportant and irrelevant in human affairs. This is atheism.[50]

Even down to spelling, students learn that personal expression, values, and ideas have become the new measuring stick.

The modern philosophy presupposes that students already possess a basic moral foundation. Modern education seeks to undermine it.

If values are relative and morals become a matter of personal preference, the entire system changes.

It brings to mind an experience I had as a student teacher years ago. Mr. B., my sixth-grade associate teacher one September, enlightened me on how he encouraged values clarification. He did not impose his beliefs or morality on others, he assured; he wanted students to form their own beliefs and value systems and take ownership of them.

This worked well for the first week, as the students appreciated the opportunity to share their own values and accept those of other classmates as unique, but neutral. These values, for the most part, were the ones they grew up with.

In the second week, one of the students decided that he didn't actually value homework and announced that he should not be expected to do any. Mr. B. pointed out that this "value" might not match others' values and therefore needed reconsideration. The rest of the students interjected with full support of the "no homework" value. Some students added that they felt a certain subject was not useful either and so shouldn't be required.

Mr. B. eventually gave a telling rebuttal. He told the students that because *he* valued homework and this particular subject, they would be required. The students could choose not to do homework elsewhere, but not in his class. He ultimately forced his morality on his students because their values did not line up with his.

If nothing is right or wrong, might becomes right.

Moral relativism is flawed at its core. It assumes that there is a neutral ground, one without judgment or forced morality. It says one can be neutral to the ideas of others, and that morality is defined as one's personal beliefs, ideas, and values. And yet this, in itself, is the push of a particular view of morality.

> The only place of true neutrality is silence. Speak up, give your opinion, contend for your view, and you forfeit your claim to neutrality.[51]

Children from Christian homes attend public schools to receive a neutral education but unknowingly become well-versed in secular philosophies. We hear it from these children as teenagers when they repeat the ideas of modern, public education that shape them—ideas that refute themselves.

1. Religion is not part of the curricula.

We ignore God, but the curricula is filled with the religion of moral relativism.

2. You can't make a judgment on others' beliefs or opinions.

You can judge someone's belief in God and his moral convictions.

3. You must tolerate everyone.

You shouldn't tolerate the people who don't tolerate something.

The lines continue to blur as moral relativism leads us further into the blindness of the myth of neutrality.

And we don't even realize how our thinking has changed.

CHAPTER 13

Myth #2: Christian School Is the Answer

Many concerned parents are choosing to leave the public school system.

In 2010, the Institute of Marriage and Family Canada released data showing a drop in public school enrolment and an increase in independent school enrolment. In September 2015, "Parents scrambl[ed] for alternatives to public schools amid [the] sex-ed row."[52]

Some look to Christian schools to provide a better grounding for their children.

But not all Christian schools are the same.

Filled with a deep commitment to the truth of Christianity, some spread Christian-ese like butter onto educational material and call it "Christian Education." Parents welcome a Bible verse at the bottom of their child's math page and believe the students are getting a truly biblical foundation.

One of our newly classically-trained students went home after the first week of school and told her mother, "The Bible is true! It's part of history! History happened in the past!" After six years in a non-classical Christian school, she was never able to make this connection before.

Inserting biblical truth into educational materials comes with the best intentions, but it misses the point.

Such shallow biblical education does not ultimately show a change in philosophy. In fact, it supports the truth of today's progressive educational agenda. The content is the same, and Christianity is sprinkled on top for a little flavouring, but it does not change the meat, or underlying philosophy.

Most of us, as parents and at work, do the same with our lives.

We separate our daily experience into sacred and secular. We bring the sacred into our work—often from guilt—but do not think deeply about what it means to have a thoroughly Christian philosophy of sales or accounting or agriculture.

We hope that by adding a little Christian-ese on top, we are being faithful.

Secularism takes the separation of sacred and secular, or "church and state," to extremes. It takes Jesus' direction to "Give to Caesar what is Caesar's and to God what is God's" far beyond its intended meaning.

Secularists not only separate Caesar and God, they publicly deny God even exists.

Secularism has taken a good thing and twisted it into something that was never intended.

Many Christians support this multi-personality view as the kind of separation Jesus taught between things of Caesar and of God. We assume that reason and revelation are two different things—two kingdoms. Biologist Steven J. Gould called them non-overlapping "magisteria."[53] We keep revelation separate and *safe* from any discussion of hard, cold facts.

Without questioning it, we are trained secularists.

We keep Christianity out of serious discussion as inappropriate or out of fear for an instant loss in credibility. If we want to sound current, we need to come across as objective, open-minded, and tolerant.

Secular thinking works to align itself with reason and science. On the side of empirical truth, it refuses to allow any ideas that cannot demonstrate their right to be in the public square based on reason and science.

The trouble is, secular thinking cannot show why it deserves this privilege. It cannot prove its own worth based on reason and science.

Secularism starts from an assumption that only reason and science deserve a voice, but it can't actually *prove* this using reason and science. Secularists set up standards for the public square that they can't live up to. They get away with it because everyone now expects that reason and science trump all, yet they don't recognize that this, in itself, is an assumption.

Classical Christian education is based on an entirely different philosophy.

It starts from the idea that we, and knowledge in general, are unified, not separate. We experience life as Christians whether it is while skating, preparing taxes, or singing in the choir. We are singular, unified individuals and believe that knowledge can, and should, be acquired as an integrated whole.

Just as we cannot have learning or knowledge without thought and understanding, classical Christian education assumes that we cannot have learning about math, science, and geography without spirituality and revelation.

As Christians, we accept much truth by revelation, but we examine and explore it all with reason and philosophy.

As Augustine wrote, "Let every good and true Christian understand that wherever truth may be found, it belongs to his Master."[54]

When we finally invite God back into the classroom and let Him shape our worldview, and as our children dig deeply into the lives and struggles of those working to understand His truth before us, our children's perspective, character, wisdom, confidence, virtue, knowledge, and understanding are changed.

Their hearts and minds are transformed forever.

They become equipped to impact both present and future generations for Jesus Christ.

CHAPTER 14

Why Classical Education May Not Be For You

While there are many reasons for choosing a classical Christian education for your children, as outlined in the previous chapters, there are also reasons why it might *not* be the best fit for your child.

1. Classical Christian education isn't specialized.

It focuses on creating thinkers who ultimately are able to work in any field, but it does not neatly package students' learning or teach them to be specialized before they know *how* to think and communicate this effectively. Classical Christian education is not eager to cut out the breadth of knowledge that the greatest thinkers throughout history had access to.

2. Classical Christian education is religious.

Classical Christian education unashamedly puts Jesus Christ in the centre of all learning. It does not claim to be neutral. It says that God is extremely relevant. It seeks to train children in the Gospel rather than having them defend what they may not grasp themselves.

3. Classical Christian education is bold.

Students educated in classical Christian schools are not afraid to be skeptical about skepticism or judgmental of more than being judgmental. They are happy to dialogue about sensitive social issues, such as quality of life and one's rights and choices, with confidence because they understand how the issues developed over time through a biblical worldview.

4. Classical Christian education is traditional.

Some parents welcome freedom in the form of a liberal education. They are not bothered by secularism, materialism, scientism, cynicism, naturalism, or socialism. Classical Christian education is very bothered by these "isms." Its focus on God's truth, beauty, goodness, and other virtues is no longer popular. Classical Christian education is only liberal in its arts, and it does not naturally embrace, but rather analyzes, current ideas.

5. Classical Christian education doesn't aim to produce wealthy, educated citizens.

Its search for truth focuses on wisdom: a better understanding of God and His purpose and will for one's short life on Earth. It does not toil only to create intellectuals who will be highly successful climbing the ladder of business or academia. Its heart is the awakening of reason, character, and spirituality in children who are able to think for themselves and eloquently and effectively communicate their ideas.

6. Classical Christian education indoctrinates children.

Classical Christian education's philosophy is intentional. Its content is well-defined. It works diligently to shape the way a child thinks and what he loves and expects to be an extension of the child's spiritual training from home.

7. Classical Christian education is all-encompassing.

It doesn't just focus on shaping the heart and mind, but also the body. Shaping hearts to follow Christ, minds to recognize truth, and bodies to become honourable temples through excellence in physical education, classical Christian education emphasizes hard work, perseverance, teamwork, and sportsmanship over individual, athletic success.

8. Classical Christian education is not the same as some other Christian schools.

It is not concerned about the Ministry of Education's expectations, because it knows it will far exceed them. It is not caught up in the latest educational methods or ideas. Instead, it holds to the same successful principles of the last several centuries.

9. Classical Christian education costs.

It is not funded by one's continually growing tax bill that only pays for modern, progressive education. It requires financial sacrifice for most, but the investment lasts for eternity.

Ultimately, where to send your children to school will shape their hearts and minds and futures . . . and subsequently our society's future too.

It's up to you.

APPENDIX A

How We Got Here in the First Place

Big ideas change society.

John Dewey was the expert behind many of the changes discussed.[55]   He wasn't the only one working to change society, but he had the biggest direct impact on education. He completely reshaped schooling in the United States in the early twentieth century, and Canada quickly followed this lead. In many ways, Dewey built on the Prussian changes designed to develop a new kind of worker, one ideally suited to power the Industrial Revolution.

But Dewey took change to a new level.

Known as the modern Aristotle, Dewey wanted ideas to be practical and useful.[56] He believed that "heavenly disagreements" caused wars, and people should focus only on practical things.

These practical things did not include God, which contributed to a shift away from a Christian education towards one which focuses on the human and material education. This included a move from intrinsic values (or things being valued as ends in themselves) to instrumental values (things being valued because they are a means).

Dewey took his passion for practicality and applied it to everything students learn in school. For example, great pieces of literature became useful to entertain or scare students into believing an idea, but nothing more. Dewey found little or no value in the character-building, training in virtue, or spiritual development usually found in great literature.

Dewey believed that education could improve society. If children were taught the right way to think, in the right kind of classroom, students would slowly change the society around them. Of course, Dewey borrowed ideas from other thinkers in his era and made room for their vision in his redesign of the classroom.

A contemporary of Dewey, Antonio Gramsci, wrote about the need for deep cultural change, a sort of evolution instead of revolution.[57] Gramsci realized that political violence could not work to change the more sophisticated, developed Western worldview, so he introduced the concept of creating a "war of position."[58]

This involved peacefully taking control of the "switch-points" of cultural values: arts and education. He suggested a "long march through the institutions" to promote a new set of standards and beliefs. The new battleground lay in schools and the traditional family, but also in churches, media, entertainment, science, literature, and civic organizations. Students needed a new social vision, thinking that dovetailed with Dewey's ideas and reduced the influence of Christianity on culture.[59]

Like Gramsci, Dewey wanted students completely engrossed in worldly thinking, in a "secular-immersion" including everything students might need to live a full life at school, work, and home.[60]

Only a uniform school system that treated everyone the same could produce the worldly thinkers Dewey wanted.

Ultimately, education needed to socialize children.

He pushed an approach to education that deliberately discouraged respect for ancient wisdom, taking for granted that the future held promise for humanity: promise of hope, kindness, and peace. Ancient stories and the study of mankind needed to be tossed away to focus on everyday needs and skills instead.

Not surprisingly, Dewey saw religion as a fuzzy collection of morals, at best. Teachers should teach religion as nothing more than superstition and the cause of war and unrest. In the twentieth century, everyone looked for ways to prevent wars.

In war-torn Europe, Gyorgy Lukacs crafted a plan to "de-Christianize Hungary."[61] He developed a "radical sex education" curriculum designed to undermine Christian ethics in order to compromise the traditional family and the Christian church. Lukacs, like Gramsci with his "march through the institutions," believed that Christianity and the West blocked the path to a new world order.[62]

In 1923, Lukacs was a founding member of the Frankfurt School, which was designed to drive social change.[63] Along with founders Herbert Marcuse and Theodor Adorno, they focused on oppressed groups to power an evolution of culture designed to transpose Marxist thought from economics into cultural terms. The Frankfurt School shaped education and academic vision during the time that Dewey wrote about education.

Dewey applied science to history and came up with scientific social studies, replacing the rich, complex dramas of history. Two thousand years of literature took a back seat to "modern," specialized courses.

Today, "modern" students learn science, history, and geography—all subjects—with hardly a passing reference to Christian faith. They might hear about the church funding exploration or building libraries to protect great literature. But students hear more about the Christian church allegedly opposing progress and academic studies than they hear about great Christian thinkers leading discoveries and scientific advance.

Modern education ultimately rewrites history in the minds of its students.

Its students learn that faith stands outside knowledge as a bystander, sometimes helpful, sometimes not.

Modern education rests on something called critical pedagogy, a combination of education and critical theory.[64] Just think of "criticism" as tearing things apart. Critical theory works to tear apart, or deconstruct, social institutions. Critical theory pulls apart history and Christianity and describes them as nothing but power struggles, or repressed desires, or oppression of minorities. Critical theory criticizes until there's nothing left to criticize.

Critical pedagogy uses this approach in the classroom. Students must unlearn, then learn and re-learn. They move through progressive cycles. Critical pedagogy rejects the idea that education should train a child to act and think like a responsible, capable adult. Instead, it sees the purpose of education to give students—indeterminate beings—a social identity without room for diversity of social opinion.

Dewey looked at socialization as the goal of "modern" education and assumed that the virtues, or pillars of our society, would always remain.

C. S. Lewis speaks to this:

> In a sort of ghastly simplicity we remove the organ and demand the function. We make men without chests and expect of them virtue and enterprise. We laugh at honour and are shocked to find traitors in our midst. We castrate and bid the geldings be fruitful.[65]

Dewey's education drowns students in slogans and popular social generalizations instead of encouraging them to develop and defend opinions of their own.

This starts right in pre-school. In some countries, nursery modern education is assumed.

> Almost every Swedish toddler heads off to preschool with trained educators, even if there is a parent still at home. (Of course, because parental leave is so generous, almost every child is cared for by their mom and dad until at least their first birthday.)[66]

As if this is enough.

Students trained by the system receive Dewey's education. Places like Germany and Sweden also make it illegal for parents to homeschool their own children, ensuring that all students receive the same message over and over again.[67]

That's "progressive" education.

But, it is not right to give Dewey too much credit for all the changes.

Others paved the way for this unprecedented change of direction in education, shaping its approach in the last century.

In order to change the worldview or "cultural hegemony" of Western civilization, the ruling influence(s) needed to be destroyed. For some, this meant the cultural hegemony of Christianity itself.

> If we repudiate liberal education, we will be saddled with illiberal education; we will exchange a disciplining of free minds for an indoctrination of servile minds.[68]

Secularists invested wholeheartedly in the shaping of ideas of future generations—generations they would never meet.

Knowing how short our lives compare with eternity, are we willing to do the same?

APPENDIX B

The Alternative

Classical education grows across North America because many realize what losing Christianity's influence means for our society's future. We have the structure, the freedoms, and the rights we have today because of our foundation. "Modern" students lack this foundation and the skills to maintain what we value most.

Classicists seek to restore them.

Classicists see learning as much more than gaining facts and skills or passing tests. These things often turn students away from true learning.

Real education rests on the training of hearts and what Susan Wise Bauer and Jessie Wise call "well-trained minds," not just gaining useful knowledge and skills.[69]

Again, classical Christian education teaches students how to think and fosters a love of learning so that they can synthesize millennia of revelation and knowledge through the lens of a Christian worldview.

As parents, we want our children to know how to use their knowledge and skills with wisdom and grace. Classicalism believes the best way to do this is by immersion in the seamless fabric of knowledge and tradition woven from the ancient world right up into modern times. It puts the twenty-five hundred years that planners such as Dewey removed back in the centre of the classroom.

Classical education serves to train disciplined minds, not to create "properly" socialized citizens.

Christian classicists believe that education aims to train minds to sense the ideal, relying on God's grace to all mankind coupled with the special grace found in the Christian revelation of Jesus.

Classical Christian education seeks to awaken and develop the best in every student rather than create identical students graduating with identical knowledge. Graduates will share a common knowledge of the basics, but they will have matured in applying the foundation to refine a rhetoric shaped by the grace God has given them as individuals. Classical education seeks to develop influencers who stand out from their public-schooled peers because they have not been trained the same way, and their unique strengths have been encouraged, developed, and rewarded.

Classical education awakens a love of learning—a passionate thirst for education for one's lifetime—that shapes students we can call truly educated. Classicists see formal education as one part of learning. But they rely on the essential role of family, Christian community, private reading, and reflection to train hearts and minds.

Along with shaping hearts to ultimately desire Jesus Christ and His kingdom, classical Christian education "endeavours to redeem the modern mind by affirming, first of all, that mind exists, and then persuading men that mind is worth possessing."[70]

Notes

[1] "John Ruskin > Quotes > Quotable Quote," GoodReads, https://www.goodreads.com/quotes/346514-the-entire-object-of-true-education-is-to-make-people.

[2] James K.A. Smith, *Desiring the Kingdom: Worship, Worldview, and Cultural Formation (Cultural Liturgies)* (Grand Rapids: Baker Academic, 2009), 25.

[3] Ibid, 27.

[4] Ibid, 25.

[5] St. Augustine, *The Confessions of Augustine, Bishop of Hippo, Book 1, Chapter 1*, http://www.leaderu.com/cyber/books/augconfessions/bk1.html.

[6] James K.A. Smith, *Desiring the Kingdom: Worship, Worldview, and Cultural Formation (Cultural Liturgies)* (Grand Rapids: Baker Academic, 2009), 57–60.

[7] Ibid, 68.

[8] Dorothy Sayers, *The Lost Tools of Learning* (La Verne, CA: Old Landmark Publishing, 1948).

⁹ Christopher Perrin, "What is Classical Education? Part III," Inside Classical Education, http://insideclassicaled.com/?p=460.

¹⁰ Ibid.

¹¹ Alvin J. Schmidt, *How Christianity Changed the World*, (Grand Rapids, MI: Zondervan, 2009), 9.

¹² Scott Masson, Email forwarded to Monica Whatley, January 22, 2016.

¹³ Susan Wise Bauer and Jessie Wise, "Great Books: A defense and the (inevitable) list," Well-Trained Mind, http://www.welltrainedmind.com/great-books/.

¹⁴ J. Warner Wallace, "Why It's Important to Inoculate (Rather Than Isolate) Our Young People," Cold-Case Christianity with J. Warner Wallace, http://coldcasechristianity.com/2013/why-its-important-to-inoculate-rather-than-isolate-our-young-people/.

¹⁵ "Unintentional Drowning: Get the Facts," Centers for Disease Control and Prevention, http://www.cdc.gov/HomeandRecreationalSafety/Water-Safety/waterinjuries-factsheet.html.

¹⁶ Susan Wise Bauer, "What is Classical Education?," Well-Trained Mind, http://www.welltrainedmind.com/classical-education/.

¹⁷ Kevin Clark and Ravi Scott Jain, *The Liberal Arts Tradition: A Philosophy of Christian Classical Education* (Camp Hill, PA: Classical Academic Press, 2013), 1.

[18] Susan Wise Bauer, "What is Classical Education?," Well-Trained Mind, http://www.welltrainedmind.com/classical-education/.

[19] Scott Masson, Email forwarded to Monica Whatley, January 22, 2016.

[20] Philip Durkin, "The Many Origins of the English Language," Slate, http://www.slate.com/blogs/lexicon_valley/2014/03/10/etymology_languages_that_have_contributed_to_english_vocabulary_over_time.html.

[21] "2014 College-Bound Seniors: Total Group Profile Report," SAT, https://secure-media.collegeboard.org/digitalServices/pdf/sat/TotalGroup-2014.pdf.

[22] Robert M. Hutchins, "The Great Conversation," The Great Ideas, http://www.thegreatideas.org/libeducation.html.

[23] Ben House, "Classical Christian Education: A Look at Some History," CRTA: Center for Reformed Theology and Apologetics, http://www.reformed.org/master/index.html?mainframe=/christian_education/classic_educ.html.

[24] E. Christian Kopff, "Greek to Us: The Death of Classical Education and Its Consequences," Taki's Magazine, http://takimag.com/article/greek_to_us_the_death_of_classical_education_and_its_consequences/print#ixzz43e2QCnaR.

[25] Carl B. Smith and Gary M. Ingersoll, "Written Vocabulary of Elementary School Pupils, Ages 6-14. Monograph in Language and Reading Studies Number 6," ERIC: Institute of Education Services, http://files.eric.ed.gov/fulltext/ED323564.pdf, 10.

[26] "OECD Skills Outlook 2013: First Results from the Survey of Adult Skills," OECD, http://skills.oecd.org/OECD_Skills_Outlook_2013.pdf, 73, 84, 93.

[27] Michael A. Woodley, Jan te Nijenhuis, and Raegan Murphy, "Were the Victorians cleverer than us? The decline in general intelligence estimated from a meta-analysis of the slowing of simple reaction time," Elsevier, https://lesacreduprintemps19.files.wordpress.com/2013/05/were-the-victorians-smarter-than-us.pdf.

[28] Will Rogers, "Will Rogers says...," Will Rogers Memorial Museums, http://www.willrogers.com/quotes.html.

[29] Glenn Reynolds, *The Education Apocalypse: How It Happened and How to Survive It,* (New York, NY: Encounter Books), 2015, accessed March 26, 2016, https://books.google.ca/books?id=rNBBCQAAQBAJ&pg=PT45&dq=The+Industrial+Revolution+created+a+need+to+educate+workers&hl=en&sa=X&ved=0ahUKEwjv0JqLn-LLAhUimoMKHd-PB2gQ6AEI-HDAA#v=onepage&q=The%20Industrial%20Revolution%20created%20a%20need%20to%20educate%20workers&f=false.

[30] J. W. Armstrong, "Examination Graduation Questions of Saline County, Kansas April 13, 1895," RootsWeb, http://www.rootsweb.ancestry.com/~kssvgs/school/exam1895/8th_exam_orig.pdf.

[31] Globe Editorial, "Ontario's sex ed teaches society's values, and that's good," The Globe and Mail, May 8, 2015, http://www.theglobeandmail.com/opinion/editorials/ontarios-sex-ed-curriculum-teaches-societys-values-and-thats-good/article24329359/.

[32] James K.A. Smith, *Desiring the Kingdom: Worship, Worldview, and Cultural Formation (Cultural Liturgies)* (Grand Rapids: Baker Academic, 2009), 40.

[33] CMEC, "CMEC Statement on Play-Based Learning," cmec: Council of Ministers of Education, Canada, http://www.cmec.ca/Publications/Lists/Publications/Attachments/282/play-based-learning_statement_EN.pdf.

[34] C. S. Lewis, *The Essential C. S. Lewis*, ed. Lyle W. Dorsett, (New York: Touchstone, 1996), 375.

[35] G. K. Chesterton, *Orthodoxy*, (Chicago: Moody Publishers, 2013).

[36] G. K. Chesterton, "Anti-Religious Thought In The 18th Century," http://www.chesterton.org/anti-religious-thought/.

[37] Art Lindsley, "C.S. Lewis on Chronological Snobbery," C. S. Lewis Institute: Knowing & Doing: A Teaching Quarterly for Discipleship of Heart and Mind, http://www.cslewisinstitute.org/webfm_send/47.

[38] Thomas Sowell, *A Conflict of Visions: Ideological Origins of Political Struggles* (New York: Basic Books, 2002).

[39] http://www.curriculum.org/secretariat/files/Dec11CharacterReport.pdf.

[40] St. Augustine, *The City of God, Books I–VII (The Fathers of the Church, Volume 8)*, 129.

[41] Geoff Beech, *Christians as Teachers: What Might It Look Like?* (Eugene, OR: Wipf and Stock, 2015).

[42] Theodore Roosevelt, "Theodore Roosevelt Quotes," Theodore Roosevelt Center,   http://www.theodorerooseveltcenter.org/Learn-About-TR/TR-Quotes.aspx.

[43] Ravi Zacharias,
https://twitter.com/ravizacharias status/483603413473587200.

[44] Timothy Dwight, *Theology: Explained and Defended, in a Series of Sermons, Volume 4* (Sagwan Press, 2015), 192.

[45] Anne F Bayefsky and Arieh Waldman, *State Support Of Religious Education: Canada Versus the United Nations (Studies in Religion, Secular Beliefs and Human Rights)* (Brill – Nijhoff, 2006), 684.

[46] OHRC, "Policy on creed and the accommodation of religious observances," Ontario Human Rights Commission, http://www.ohrc.on.ca/sites/default/files/attachments/Policy_on_creed_and_the_accommodation_of_religious_observances.pdf.

[47] Dakshana Bascaramurty and Joe Friesen, "Canadian schools struggle with what to do about Christmas," The Globe and Mail, http://www.theglobeandmail.com/life/holiday-guide/canadian-schools-struggle-with-what-to-do-about-christmas/article1357339/.

[48] Charles Lewis, "Muslim prayers during class time draws fire at Toronto school," National Post, http://news.nationalpost.com/holy-post/muslim-prayers-during-class-time-draws-fire-at-toronto-school.

[49] Milton Friedman and Rose Friedman, *Free to Choose: A Personal Statement* (New York: Mariner Books, 1990), 164.

[50] Gordon H. Clark, ed. John W. Robbins, "A Christian Philosophy of Education," The Trinity Review (Unicoi, TN: May, June 1988), 5.

[51] Greg Koukl, "The Myth of Moral Neutrality," Stand to Reason, http://www.str.org/articles/the-myth-of-moral-neutrality#.VVC4nNpVikp.

[52] Noor Javed and Kristin Rushowy, "Parents scrambling for alternatives to public schools amid sex-ed row," TheStar, https://beta.thestar.com/yourtoronto/education/2015/09/03/parents-scrambling-for-alternatives-to-public-schools-amid-sex-ed-row.html.

[53] Stephen Jay Gould, "Nonoverlapping Magisteria," The Unofficial Stephen Jay Gould Archive, http://www.stephenjaygould.org/library/gould_noma.html.

[54] St. Augustine, *On Christian Doctrine Book II 18.28.*

[55] John Dewey, "The educational situation: As concerns the public schools," Taylor Francis, Journal of Curriculum Studies, http://www.tandfonline.com/doi/abs/10.1080/00220270010023803.

[56] http://digitalcommons.law.yale.edu/cgi/viewcontent cgi?article=5106&context=fss_papers.

[57] Roberta Robaina, "Gramsci and revolution: a necessary clarification," http://isj.org.uk/gramsci-and-revolution-a-necessary-clarification/.

[58] Ibid.

[59] Tracey Rowland, "Comunione e Liberazione: Christ and culture in the contest between Giussani and Gramsci," ABC (Australian Broadcasting Company) Religion and Ethics, http://www.abc.net.au/religion/articles/2013/03/25/3723165.htm.

[60] Andrew Hartman, "Is Secular Humanism a Religion?" Society for U.S. Intellectual History, http://s-usih.org/2011/02/is-secular-humanism-religion.html.

[61] Linda Kimball, "Cultural Marxism," American Thinker, http://www.americanthinker.com/articles/2007/02/cultural_marxism.html.

[62] Ibid.

[63] Claudio Corradetti, "The Frankfurt School and Critical Theory," Internet Encyclopedia of Philosophy, http://www.iep.utm.edu/frankfur/.

[64] Tait Coles,"Critical pedagogy: schools must equip students to challenge the status quo," The Guardian, http://www.theguardian.com/teacher-network/teacher-blog/2014/feb/25/critical-pedagogy-schools-students-challenge.

[65] C. S. Lewis, *The Abolition of Man* (New York: Touchstone, 1996), 37.

[66] Erin Anderssen, "What the world can teach Canada about building better daycare," The Globe and Mail, http://www.theglobeandmail.com/life/parenting/what-the-world-can-teach-canada-about-building-better-daycare/article15036667/?page=all.

[67] Alycia Bayer, "Which countries have banned homeschooling?" Examiner. com, http://www.examiner.com/article/which-countries-have-banned-homeschooling.

[68] *Russell Kirk, Prospects for Conservatives: A Compass for Rediscovering the Permanent Things* (Imaginative Conservative Books, 2013), 49.

[69] Susan Wise Bauer and Jessie Wise, *The Well-Trained Mind: A Guide to Classical Education at Home (Third Edition)* (New York: W. W. Norton and Co.: 2009).

[70] Russell Kirk, *Prospects for Conservatives: A Compass for Rediscovering the Permanent Things* (Imaginative Conservative Books, 2013), 56.

Acknowledgements

A project like this is not possible without the help and support of many.

First of all, thanks to Dr. Craig Carter who initially helped us realize our task was far more important than we had ever imagined.

Thank you also to those who read the drafts and added their great ideas to the book's development:

> Tim Barnett, David Brewer, Kevin Clark, Ryan Eras, Dr. Bill Friesen, Reni Horban, Dr. Scott Masson, and Elaine Philip.

Each of your astute recommendations was invaluable and gave this message strength.

This book's cover looks beautiful thanks to Hilary McLaughlin, photographer, and to students, T. G. and E. A., whose faces capture our purpose perfectly.

A special thanks to Dave Jumaquio for his exceptional cover design and interior formatting.

Gifted editor, Blake Atwood, improved the manuscript tremendously by catching so many little errors. Thank you for all your support with the notes page, especially.

Thanks to the staff at Innova Academy, especially Beth Brewer and Adele McLaughlin, for moral support when there was so much else to do. And to Adele for using your skills to do a thorough edit.

Thank you also to my siblings, Marina Walker, Michelle Montemurro, Marla Klinck, my mother, Erin Giardetti, and Shawn's parents, Dan and Arlene Whatley, who graciously read and offered parents' perspectives. Your comments brought life to the content.

A special thank you to the largest contributor to this book, Keith King. Way back in that coffee shop, where we scribbled early concepts on that napkin, a great purpose became clear. Thank you for your continual support throughout every facet of this endeavour. You have been so instrumental in this project and have not wavered from your desire to get this message out. And behind every great man is a great woman; thank you, Janine King, for your gracious care—from your countless reads to your personal words of encouragement when the undertaking grew.

Thank you to our four children, Lara, Kate, Jonathan, and Emma, for your tremendous patience as we wrote one more page of "that book." You are so very precious to us. This story is for parents of children like you.

Without the investment of Shawn, this was impossible. Thank you for the many pages (especially Appendix A) that clearly reflect your genius; God has gifted you with a brilliant mind. Your understanding of the philosophies that shape our current culture and your ability to express this eloquently and effectively are pivotal to truly grasping our urgency.

Most importantly, we thank God for helping us in this seemingly impossible task—for using us, as unequipped as we are, to share this truth with others.